HEALING SOMATIC TRAUMA

A Step by Step Guide to Simple Techniques for Stress Relief and Building Body-Mind Connections

Dr. Lizzy Darlington

a particular purpose. No warranty may be created or extended by sales representatives or written sales materials. The advice and strategies contained herein may not be suitable for your situation. You should consult with a professional when appropriate. Neither the publisher nor the author shall be liable for any loss of profit or any other commercial damages, including but not limited to special, incidental, consequential, personal, or other damages.

Table of contents

Preface

Embracing and Understanding Somatic Trauma

Imagine carrying a rucksack full of stones, each symbolising a stressful or painful event in your life. With each stride, the weight pounds down, serving as a persistent reminder of painful times. This is what somatic trauma may feel like: a bodily load from mental scars.

You may not even be aware of the burden you are carrying. It has ingrained itself in you, affecting your behaviours and emotions in subtle ways. But what if you could put the backpack down? What if you could move freely again?

Personal Stories of Healing

Let us discuss Anna. She was always on edge, snapping at her loved ones, and couldn't understand why. It wasn't until she started somatic therapy that she discovered her body was still carrying the stress of a vehicle accident from years earlier. She learnt to listen to her body's messages and react compassionately via guided exercises. Slowly, the tension dissipated, and she experienced a feeling of serenity she hadn't felt in years.

Then there's David, who had dreams that left him fatigued every morning. He felt unconnected from his body and went through life as if on autopilot. Somatic treatment taught him how to ground himself, feel his feet on the ground, and breathe in rhythm. As he grew more present in his body, the nightmares faded and comfortable sleep returned.

These tales are not unusual. They are reflected in the lives of numerous others who have found the effectiveness of healing somatic trauma. It is a path of reconnecting with oneself and going within to repair bodily hurts.

Importance of Addressing Somatic Trauma

You may be wondering why it is so important to cope with somatic trauma. It's because your body remembers. Every shock, harsh remark, and loss is imprinted on your muscles and nerves. If neglected, these memories might manifest as persistent pain, worry, and depression. They may prevent you from living the life you deserve.

Addressing somatic trauma is about more than just symptom relief; it's about regaining your life. It's about waking up every day feeling lighter and more energised to follow your dreams. It's about enjoying times with loved ones without the weight of prior anguish hanging over you.

When you begin to recover somatically, you are not just working through emotional wounds, but also developing resilience. You're learning to listen to your body's wisdom, realise when you're about to reach your limitations, and take actions to care for yourself. This self-awareness is a strong weapon that can help you navigate life's problems with grace and courage.

If you are reading this, now is the moment to take the first move. Whether you're suffering with the repercussions of a single tragedy or a lifetime of stress, remember that it's never too late to begin healing. There are tools accessible, specialists educated to advise you, and a network of individuals who have travelled this road before you.

As you read this book, have an open mind and heart. The activities and ideas presented here are more than simply words; they are keys to living a more vivid, satisfying life. Every chapter is an invitation to discover, learn, and develop.

Remember that healing is not a linear process. There may be ups and downs, but every stride forward is a success. Be patient with yourself, and appreciate minor victories. You are on your way to becoming the finest version of yourself, free of the burdens of the past and open to the present and future.

So take a big breath. You are about to embark on a fantastic trip. A journey of healing, discovery, and, finally, liberation. Welcome to the road of somatic healing.

Introduction

Trauma is a term that generally conjures up images of emotional wounds, but it refers to more than that. Somatic trauma is the kind of trauma that becomes ingrained in your body rather than simply your memory. It's like a shadow that follows you, influencing your feelings and actions without your knowledge.

What Is Somatic Trauma?

Somatic trauma happens when stressful events become ingrained in your body. Consider your body to be a sponge that absorbs all of your life's difficulties. These might be major catastrophes such as accidents or losses, or minor, repetitive pressures that accumulate over time. Your body remembers these events, which might manifest as tension, discomfort, or even certain disorders.

Impact on Body and Mind

When your body clings onto trauma, it may alter the way you live. You may feel nervous or sad, unable to sleep, or isolated from your surroundings. It's as if your body is always on high alert, ready to defend you from danger even when there is none. This may be tiresome and interfere with one's enjoyment of life.

Somatic trauma may also have an impact on your mental health. You may have difficulty focusing or find yourself repeatedly recalling the stressful experience. It might seem like you're locked in a cycle, unable to progress.

An overview of somatic healing.

Somatic healing is all about assisting your body in letting go of trauma. It's a method of paying attention to what your body is telling you and reacting with compassion. There are several methods to do this, all of them require reconnecting with your body.

One approach is to relocate. This might include mild workouts, dancing, or just stretching. The goal is to assist your body release the stress it's been hanging onto.

Another way is mindfulness, which involves paying attention to the current moment. This may help you become more aware of your body's signals and learn how to react to them in a healthy manner.

Breathing exercises are also an important component of somatic healing. They may quiet your nervous system and allow your body to relax.

Working with a therapist to take you through these techniques and help you comprehend your sensations is another option for somatic recovery.

The Path Ahead

Recovery from somatic trauma is a process. It won't happen quickly, but with patience and effort, you may begin to feel better. You'll learn how to listen to and care for your body. You'll discover new techniques to relieve the pain and tension that have been holding you down.

As you read this book, you will learn more about somatic trauma and how to recover from it. You'll discover activities and practices that may help you feel better. You will also hear experiences from people who have been in your situation and found a way out.

Remember that recovery is possible. It takes time and work, but the results are worthwhile. You deserve to be in excellent physical and mental health. So, take a big breath, and let's start this trip together.

Part 1 : Understanding Somatic Trauma.

The Science of Trauma

When something really frightening or painful occurs, it may leave an imprint not just on your mind, but also on your body. This is what we call trauma. It's as if your body and brain recall unpleasant things and continue to experience it, even after the threat has passed.

Assume you're going through the woods and see a bear. Your heart beats quickly, your muscles tighten, and you become very alert. That is your body's alarm system, known as the nervous system, responding to safeguard you. It prepares you to either flee or fend off the bear.

If you are unable to escape or fight, such as in a life-threatening scenario, your body may continue to be on high alert. Later on, things that remind you of that terrifying event might cause your body to respond as if the bear is there again, even if it's simply a picture of a bear or a similar sound.

This is because your neurological system has altered. It's as if it's grown incredibly skilled at ringing the alarm—perhaps too good. So today, even little incidents might make you feel like you're in serious danger. This might make you feel exhausted, worried, or injured without any apparent cause.

But here's the good news: just as your body learnt to be hyper-vigilant, it can learn to relax and feel secure again. This is exactly what somatic healing is about. It's like persuading your body that the bear is gone and everything is OK. You may do this by doing exercises that help you sense where your body's stress is and gradually release it.

Understanding somatic trauma is studying how your body copes with adversity and how to help it recall how to be peaceful and joyful again. It's a significant step toward feeling healthier and enjoying life more.

Biological and psychological consequences of trauma

Trauma may have a wide range of physical and mental effects. Biologically, when you experience extreme stress, your body responds by producing stress chemicals such as adrenaline and cortisol. This is part of the "fight or flight" reaction, which your body uses to prepare for danger. If the stress is excessive or prolonged, these hormones may continue to flow in your body, causing headaches, difficulty sleeping, and even cardiac problems.

Psychologically, trauma may disrupt your feelings and thinking. You may often experience feelings of fear, sadness, or anger. It might be difficult to focus or recall information. Some individuals may experience numbness or disconnection from the world around them. Even when you're secure, trauma may leave you feeling on edge, as if something horrible is about to happen.

The biological and psychological repercussions of trauma are linked. For example, if your body is always tight due to stress hormones, you may feel apprehensive or concerned. If you're feeling dejected or worried, your body may get fatigued or achy.

The good news is that there are strategies to help your body and mind heal from trauma. Therapy, exercise, and talking to someone you trust may all make a significant effect. It's vital to remember that healing takes time, and it's OK to seek support along the road.

The nerve system and traumatic response

When you go through anything really difficult, such as a terrifying accident or a significant loss, your nervous system, which functions as the body's alarm system, goes into overdrive. This system has a large responsibility: it keeps you safe by preparing you to meet danger. It is what causes you to leap out of the path of a speeding bike or makes your pulse beat when you are anxious.

Here's how it works: your nervous system's stress response is divided into two major components. The sympathetic nervous system functions similarly to a car's gas pedal. It hurries things up and prepares you to fight or flee. When you're terrified, your breathing quickens and your muscles tense up.

The second portion is the parasympathetic nervous system, which functions similarly to the brake. It helps you calm down and relax when the threat has passed. It allows you to take a deep breath and feel peaceful again.

However, if the trauma is severe or repeated, your nervous system may get stuck in high gear. It's as if the throttle pedal is jammed, and you can't locate the brake. This might make you feel nervous, jumpy, or have trouble sleeping. It's your body's attempt to protect you, but it may be quite difficult to live like this all the time.

The good news is that you can train your nervous system to locate the brake again. Deep breathing, muscular relaxation, and certain sorts of treatment may all help your body relearn how to calm down. It's like retraining your body's alarm system to stop going off all the time. This may help you feel less stressed and more like yourself again.

History of Somatic Therapy

Somatic therapy is a distinct kind of treatment that acknowledges the profound relationship between the mind and the body. Its origins may be traced back to the nineteenth century, with the advent of physical education movements such as yoga, pilates, and judo. These activities paved the way for what would eventually become known as somatic therapy.

The name "somatic" is derived from the Greek word "soma," which means "living body." Somatic therapy focuses on the body's involvement in emotions and experiences, particularly in relation to trauma and stress. It's all about recognizing how your body stores emotions and finding strategies to release them.

Wilhelm Reich, Sigmund Freud's pupil, was a pioneering figure in somatic therapy. In the 1930s, Reich hypothesised that trauma might cause bodily symptoms such as muscular tension and discomfort. He felt that suppressed emotions might form a "body armour" that shields us from previous painful events but also prevents us from fully experiencing our current feelings.

Later, in the 1970s, a philosopher and movement theorist named Thomas Hanna expanded on the notion of somatics. He characterised it as an experiential study of the body, stressing the role of human experience and consciousness in healing.

Somatic therapy combines physical and conversation therapy to assist patients become conscious of their suppressed thoughts and feelings. It aids in stress management and the recovery from stressful events. The theory is that by being more aware of your body and its functions, you may uncover unconscious signals and overcome trauma-induced blocks.

Today, somatic therapy employs a number of practices, including breathwork, movement, and touch, to assist patients in connecting with their bodies and healing from trauma. It is a holistic approach that takes into account the whole individual - mind, body, and spirit - on the path to wellbeing.

Evolution of Somatic Practices

Somatic techniques have developed throughout time, combining traditional knowledge and contemporary science. The trip started with centuries-old disciplines such as yoga and martial arts. These practices emphasised the relationship between mind and body, helping individuals to become more aware of their bodily feelings and emotions.

A change happened throughout the late nineteenth and early twentieth century. People such as Genevieve Stebbins in the United States and Elsa Gindler in Europe began to create novel approaches to studying bodily awareness. They were inspired by the physical culture movement, which included exercise, dance, and gymnastics.

Philosophers such as John Dewey and Rudolf Steiner also had an impact. They believed in learning via experience, which influenced how somatic techniques were taught. Dancers such as Isadora Duncan and Rudolf von Laban deviated from conventional dance patterns, resulting in more expressive movements that matched the body's inherent rhythms.

The early pioneers of somatic techniques, such as Frederick Matthias Alexander, Moshe Feldenkrais, and Ida Rolf, were motivated by personal injuries and a desire to avoid them. They created strategies that not only aided in recuperation, but also improved bodily awareness and well-being.

Throughout the twentieth century, the pioneers' pupils developed and taught these principles. They formed important schools and styles, which helped to disseminate knowledge of somatic techniques even farther. Today, somatic activities are employed in psychotherapy, dance, and spiritual development to help individuals reconnect with their bodies and recover from traumas.

The emergence of somatic practices demonstrates a rising acknowledgment of the body's importance in our overall health and pleasure. It's a discipline that's always evolving, providing fresh insights into how we might live more happily with our bodies.

Key people and their contributions

Several notable personalities have contributed significantly to the area of somatic therapy, each with their own set of thoughts and methodologies. Here are some of them:

- **Wilhelm Reich**: Known as the "Father of Somatic Therapy," Reich was a disciple of Freud who thought that psychological difficulties might emerge physically. He proposed the notion of "character armour," which holds that humans form a physical shell to shield themselves from emotional anguish.

- **Pierre Janet:** A French psychotherapist, Janet made important advances to our knowledge of the body's role in mental health. He investigated how previous traumas could impact people's current physical status.

- **Thomas Hanna:** Hanna invented the word "somatics" in the 1970s, emphasising the role of bodily awareness and movement in healing. He invented Hanna Somatic Education, a technique for re-educating the body to move more freely and relieve chronic pain.

- Moshe Feldenkrais: The founder of the Feldenkrais Method, he created a technique that enhances movement and function via awareness. His approach has assisted many individuals in overcoming pain and mobility concerns.

- Ida Rolf, the pioneer of Rolfing, created a kind of deep tissue massage that aligns the body and improves posture. Her study has influenced our knowledge of the body's structure and capability for change.

- Peter Levine: Based on his studies of animals' reactions to dangers, Levine created Somatic Experiencing, a technique for treating trauma symptoms by concentrating on physical sensations.

These pioneers, among others, helped form our understanding of the mind-body relationship, and their work continues to impact current somatic therapies.

Types of Somatic Trauma

Somatic trauma may take many forms, and recognizing them can help you discover the best method to recover. Experts have created the following forms of somatic trauma therapy:

1. Standard Somatic Experiencing: This method helps you move through trauma by concentrating on your body's experiences. It was developed by Peter Levine, who witnessed how animals naturally relieve tension and wanted to assist people do the same.

2. Sensorimotor Psychotherapy: This approach combines somatic treatment and psychotherapy. It allows you to identify and adjust your bodily reactions to trauma.

3. The Hakomi Method: This gentle approach mixes Western psychology with Eastern philosophy. It employs mindfulness to help you understand how your body stores trauma.

4. Bioenergetic Therapy: This approach believes that emotional difficulties may generate physical strain. It includes activities to help you relieve stress and express your emotions.

5. Biodynamic Psychotherapy: This treatment emphasises the relationship between your body, mind, and soul. It helps you recover from trauma via breathing and movement.

6. Brainspotting: This technique is based on the theory that where you look influences how you feel. It assists you in processing trauma by identifying areas in your visual field that correspond to emotional suffering.

Each of these treatments has a unique approach to helping you connect with your body in order to recover from trauma. It's all about determining which one is ideal for you and your quest to feel better.

Acute, chronic, and complicated trauma.

Trauma may be a very upsetting or unsettling event. It is classified into three types: acute, chronic, and complex trauma. Here's a quick summary of each:

- **Acute Trauma:** Caused by a single stressful or hazardous incident, such as a natural catastrophe, vehicle accident, or attack.

- **Chronic Trauma:** This is defined as frequent and sustained exposure to very stressful situations, such as child abuse, bullying, or domestic violence.

- **Complex Trauma:** Often caused by exposure to several traumatic incidents, and it is often interpersonal, including direct damage, exploitation, and mistreatment like abuse or extreme neglect.

Understanding the subtleties of various trauma types is critical for providing effective therapy and support. If you or someone you know is experiencing trauma, seeking professional treatment from a therapist or counsellor might be useful.

Trauma at various life phases

Trauma may strike at any time in life, and its effects vary depending on the individual's age, development, and support systems available. Here's how trauma may influence people at various life stages:

- **Infancy and Early Childhood:** Trauma at this time may undermine attachment and trust, thereby impairing learning and social interaction.

- **Middle childhood trauma:** This may have an impact on self-esteem, academic achievement, and peer relationships. Children may experience dread, anxiety, and behavioural issues.

- **Adolescence:** Trauma may interfere with identity development and self-image, leading to risky behaviours or drug misuse.

- **In adulthood**, trauma may have an influence on relationships, job performance, and general well-being. Adults may have a variety of emotional reactions, such as despair and PTSD.

- **Older Adulthood**: Trauma may increase health issues, cause emotions of powerlessness, and impair memory and cognition.

Trauma recovery is often a multi-stage process that includes treatment, support groups, and self-care practices. It is critical to seek professional assistance if trauma is hurting one's life.

Part II: Somatic Healing Techniques

Principles of Somatic Healing.

Somatic healing, often known as somatic therapy, is a holistic approach that focuses on the body-mind link. It is founded on the belief that trauma and stress may appear physically in the body. Here are a few fundamental ideas of somatic healing:

- **Body-Mind Connection:** Recognizes how our physical experiences and emotions are linked. This idea is crucial to understanding how the body stores and expresses emotional events.

- **Grounding:** Making physical touch with the earth's surface to relieve inflammation, discomfort, and tension. It's a strategy for helping people feel more present and connected to their surroundings.

- **Boundary Development:** Emphasises understanding and respecting the physical and emotional boundaries between oneself and others. This is especially crucial for those who have been traumatised and may have lost their sense of limits.

- **Self-Regulation:** teaches how to control overwhelming emotions caused by painful memories. This is critical to avoiding re-traumatization throughout the healing process.

- **Movement and Process:** Physical movement is used to aid with emotional processing and release. This may involve touch, massage, breathing methods, and other types of bodywork.

- **Sequencing:** The process of releasing memories held in the body, which may assist relieve muscular tension and return the neurological system to a more balanced condition.

Somatic healing may help people cope with a variety of ailments, including stress, sorrow, anxiety, depression, and post-traumatic stress disorder (PTSD). It's a kind of therapy that helps individuals become more aware of their physiological sensations and learn to feel secure in their bodies while examining ideas, emotions, and memories.

Safety, connectivity, and regulation.

Safety, connection, and regulation are critical components in trauma recovery. Here's a quick overview of each:

- **Safety:** Creating a feeling of safety is the first stage in trauma rehabilitation. It entails providing a safe atmosphere and a feeling of internal safety in which individuals may begin to process traumatic events without fear of harm.

- **Connection:** Recovering from trauma often requires supportive connections and a feeling of belonging with others. This may include friends, family, therapists, or support groups who provide empathy, understanding, and affirmation.

- **Regulation:** The capacity to control one's emotions and physiological conditions. Self-regulation techniques assist people in dealing with and reducing the severity of traumatic stress reactions.

These concepts are part of a larger therapeutic strategy that stresses the necessity of treating the physical, emotional, and relational elements of trauma in order to enable a whole healing process. Co-regulation, or engaging with others to assist manage emotional states, is also an important part of this process. Individuals suffering from trauma should consult with specialists who can help them through the phases of recovery.

The significance of the therapist-client interaction

The therapist-client interaction is an essential component of trauma rehabilitation. It is based on trust, mutual respect, and cooperation, and provides a secure environment for the client to examine and process traumatic events. Here are some important details concerning its involvement in trauma healing:

- **Trust and Safety:** A healthy therapeutic connection fosters a feeling of trust and safety, allowing clients to feel comfortable discussing their experiences and vulnerabilities.

- **Empowerment:** Through this connection, therapists empower clients by validating their experiences and assisting them on their road to healing and resilience.

- **Attachment and Connection**: A strong therapy connection may help clients recover emotionally, especially if they have had attachment disturbances or interpersonal traumas.

- **Tailored Approach:** Therapists strive to understand each client's unique requirements, adapting their approach to the individual's personal condition, background, and objectives.

- **Co-regulation:** The therapy relationship may also serve as a model for good interpersonal relationships, teaching clients how to manage their emotions and form connections with others.

Overall, the therapeutic alliance is more than simply a setting for implementing procedures; it is an active and important element of the healing process.

Core Somatic Practices.

Core somatic practices are therapeutic procedures that use the body's own experiences to promote healing and wellbeing. Here are a few crucial practices:

- **Diaphragmatic Breathing:** This technique uses deep breathing via the diaphragm to enhance relaxation and relieve tension.

- **Grounding exercises** are techniques that help people connect with the present moment and feel more secure and focused in their bodies.

- **Pelvic Tilts**: A movement exercise in which the pelvis is gently rocked forward and backward to raise awareness of the pelvic area and release stress.

- **Shoulder Rolls:** Rolling the shoulders relieves tension and increases awareness of how the body stores stress.

- **Somatic Experiencing:** Peter Levine created this body-focused treatment to assist relieve the physical tension associated with trauma without immediately triggering unpleasant memories.

These activities attempt to increase bodily awareness, relieve tension, and improve emotional control. They may be especially beneficial for those healing from trauma and stress-related disorders. It is critical to participate in these activities under the supervision of a skilled practitioner, particularly when coping with trauma.

Grounding and Centering

Grounding and centering are practices for returning oneself to the present moment, particularly while feeling overwhelmed or detached. Here are some grounding and centering practices that may be useful:

Grounding Techniques:

1. Physical Sensation: Concentrate on the physical sensations in your body, such as the feel of your feet on the ground or the texture of an item in your hands.

2. Breathing Exercises: Practise deep breathing by gently inhaling through your nose and expelling through your mouth.

3. Technique: 5-4-3-2-1: Identify five visible objects, four tactile objects, three auditory objects, two olfactory objects, and one gustatory object.

4. Nature Connection: To feel more grounded, spend time in nature and touch the soil or plants.

Centering Techniques:

1. Visualisation: Imagine a line flowing down the centre of your body, connecting you to the ground.

2. Posture: To feel more centred, stand or sit straight, keeping your head, neck, and spine aligned.

3. Movement: Gentle motions such as tai chi or yoga might help you relax and centre yourself.

4. Mindfulness. Meditation is concentrating on the current moment and monitoring your thoughts and emotions without judgement.

These approaches are adaptable to any lifestyle and are especially beneficial for controlling anxiety, panic, trauma, and stress. It's important to locate the ones that work best for you and practise them often.

Breathing techniques and sensory awareness

Breathwork and sensory awareness are essential components of many mindfulness and stress-reduction techniques. Focusing on the breath helps to regulate the nervous system and promote awareness of the current moment. Here's a quick overview:

Breathwork aims to improve health and well-being via mindful breathing techniques.

- Can reduce acute stress responses and avoid chronic stress-related health issues.

- Deep abdominal breathing promotes the body's relaxation response, which lowers blood pressure and improves circulation.

- Regular practice may increase energy, improve immunity, and aid with pain management.

- Mindful breathing may boost mood and help those with depression by anchoring them in the present moment.

Sensory Awareness refers to the aware experience of our senses, including sight, hearing, touch, taste, and smell.

- Helps us focus our attention on the present moment, which may be relaxing and grounding.

- Sensory exercises, such as the 5-4-3-2-1 approach, may help to reduce anxiety and tension.

- Concentrating on the breath may activate neuronal networks outside of the brain stem that are associated with emotion, attention, and bodily awareness, giving a tool for stress regulation.

These routines benefit both mental and physical health, enhancing mood, sleep quality, respiratory function, and general well-being. It is best to participate in these techniques under the supervision of a skilled practitioner, particularly when coping with trauma or stress-related disorders.

Movement-Based Therapy

Movement-based treatments are a class of therapy approaches that use movement to improve physical, mental, and emotional health. Here's a summary of what they include and how they might be useful:

- **Improving Well-Being:** Movement-based treatments attempt to improve a person's cognitive, physical, mental, and emotional well-being.

- **Expression via Movement:** They encourage people to express their emotions, thoughts, and ideas via physical movement in a secure setting.

- **Neuroplasticity:** Movement is an important trigger for neuroplasticity, which is the brain's capacity to establish and restructure synaptic connections, particularly in response to learning, experience, or damage.

- **Diverse Techniques:** Movement-based treatments include Dance Therapy, Rhythmic Movement Therapy, Brain Gym, and Functional Neurology techniques.

- **Accessibility:** Movement therapy is beneficial to anybody who wants to connect with their body and better understand themselves.

Movement-based treatments may be especially beneficial for those who are healing from trauma, struggling with stress-related diseases, or looking to enhance their general well-being. It is advised that you participate in these procedures under the supervision of a certified practitioner.

Movement therapy, such as yoga and dance.

Yoga, dancing, and other movement therapies are examples of holistic healing techniques that combine the body and mind to enhance overall health and well-being. Here's a quick summary of each:

- **Yoga** is a mind-body discipline that includes physical postures, breathing exercises, meditation, and ethical guidelines. Its advantages include greater flexibility, better respiratory and cardiovascular function, more balanced metabolism, and higher overall vitality.

- **Dance therapy**, also known as dance/movement therapy (DMT), is a psychotherapy approach that uses movement to achieve emotional, social, cognitive, and physical integration. It may enhance cognitive performance, emotional well-being, and behaviour, making it an effective tool in psychiatric therapy.

Other movement therapies, such as tai chi, Pilates, Feldenkrais Method, and Alexander Technique, aim to improve movement patterns, body awareness, and alignment for optimal health and function.

These treatments may be especially effective for those who want to recover from trauma, manage stress, improve mental health, or just improve their physical well-being. It is critical to participate in these activities under the supervision of a skilled practitioner, particularly when dealing with specific health concerns.

Adapting movement to individual requirements.

Individualising movement is a tailored strategy that takes into account each person's unique physical and mental characteristics. Here are some significant features of this approach:

- **Assessment:** Understanding the individual's existing physical condition, activity habits, and personal aspirations is critical. This may include a thorough health history, physical exams, and conversations about individual preferences.

- **Customization:** Based on the evaluation, a personalised movement plan is developed. This might include particular workouts, adaptations, and progressions that are tailored to the individual's physique and goals.

- **Integration:** The strategy should be incorporated into the individual's daily routine. This includes considerations such as time limits, limited resources, and other obligations.

- **Adaptability:** As the person develops or their demands change, the mobility plan should be flexible. This guarantees that the strategy is both relevant and effective.

- **Holistic Approach:** It is important to address not just the physical elements, but also the emotional and psychological consequences of movement. The strategy should promote general well-being.

By concentrating on these factors, movement may be adjusted to match specific requirements, resulting in more productive and pleasurable experiences. A tailored approach may make a huge impact in rehabilitation, fitness, and overall health.

Touch & Bodywork

Touch and bodywork are therapeutic methods that use physical touch or manipulation of the body to promote healing, relaxation, and overall well-being. Here is a summary of these practices:

- **NeuroAffective Touch:** This kind of bodywork combines touch with psychotherapy to treat emotional, relational, and developmental issues. It is very effective for healing trauma that cannot be touched via verbal techniques alone.

- **Trauma-Informed Bodywork:** This method to touch therapy is tailored to the requirements of those who have experienced trauma. It allows clients to reclaim agency over touch and their bodies, which aids in the discharge of trauma trapped inside the body.

- **Touch and Awareness Bodywork:** This intuitive practice focuses on reducing tension and enhancing vitality via touch. It is founded on the idea that the body has profound insights into our experiences and emotions.

- **Integrated Touch Body Work:** This sort of bodywork may include treatments such as waxing and body contouring, which may improve a person's overall well-being and body image.

These techniques are often used in combination with other types of treatment and may be especially beneficial for those healing from physical or mental trauma. To guarantee a safe and beneficial experience, consult with competent individuals who have been educated in these approaches.

The importance of touch in healing

Touch has an important and diverse function in healing, including physiological, psychological, and neurological aspects. Here's a summary of how touch promotes healing:

- **Physiological Impact:** Touch may cause the release of oxytocin, sometimes known as the "love hormone," which decreases stress, lowers blood pressure, and promotes feelings of trust and emotional attachment. It also causes the production of endorphins, the body's natural painkillers, which may help relieve pain and increase overall well-being.

- **Psychological Benefits:** Touch is essential for developing and sustaining relationships. It may make people feel more connected, understood, and supported, thereby enhancing mental health and decreasing feelings of social isolation and loneliness, particularly among older folks.

- **Neurological Mechanisms:** Touch sensations are processed by specialised nerve receptors in the skin, which convey messages to the brain, eliciting emotional and physiological responses. C-tactile afferents, a kind of nerve fibre, are hypothesised to play an important role in the emotional and social elements of touch by linking to brain locations that process emotions.

- **Therapeutic Applications:** In the context of healthcare, touch fosters a healing link, which is especially important in our more hands-off, impersonal age. For thousands of years, it has been acknowledged as a fundamental component of the healing arts, with touch-based techniques such as massage therapy, Reiki, and other types of bodywork utilised to help with pain treatment, stress reduction, and relaxation.

- **Contact Deprivation:** A lack of contact might be harmful to your health. Touch is essential for survival, as shown by studies on the development of young monkeys and human neonates. "Kangaroo care" for newborns, which includes skin-to-skin contact, reduces the rate at which blood infections occur.

Incorporating touch into healing techniques may improve the therapeutic experience and aid in physical and emotional rehabilitation. It is crucial to stress that, although touch has numerous advantages, it should always be used in a way that respects the recipient's comfort and limits.

Boundaries and ethical issues

Boundaries and ethical concerns are essential in therapy engagements to preserve clients' well-being and professional integrity. Here are some important points:

- **Beneficence**: Therapists must advocate what is best for their clients, with the assumption that they will benefit from the sessions.

- **Nonmaleficence:** The concept of "doing no harm" is most important. Therapists must avoid doing activities that might hurt the client.

- **Autonomy**: Therapists should foster clients' autonomous thinking and decision-making while discouraging any type of reliance.

- **Boundary Management:** Boundaries might include touch, time, distance, gifts, and self-disclosure. Managing these limits effectively is critical for the client's well-being and good therapeutic results.

- **Ethical Practice:** Therapists must use their judgement to determine the acceptability of certain acts and behaviours, drawing on ethical guidelines and consulting with others.

These principles contribute to the development of a therapeutic framework that specifies responsibilities for participants in the therapeutic process, encouraging a feeling of safety and trust in the therapist to always act in the client's best interests. Therapists must be aware of and follow these ethical principles in order to deliver effective and ethical therapy.

Part III: Mindfulness and Emotional Regulation

Mindfulness in Somatic Healing.

Imagine you're on an inside excursion, with your own body serving as the scenery. In the world of somatic healing, mindfulness serves as a compass, leading you through the feelings, emotions, and experiences that exist inside. As you focus your attention within, you start to notice the tiny murmurs of your body, the stiffness in your shoulders, the flutter of anxiousness in your stomach, or the warmth of happiness in your chest.

In this aware state, you are more than simply a passive spectator; you are actively involved in your inner environment. Each breath serves as a bridge between your conscious mind and the bodily feelings that sometimes go undetected. This steady, regular breath serves as a tool for study and discovery. It enables you to explore the depths of your being, to touch the areas that have been injured, and to provide the healing balm of consciousness.

As you practise mindfulness in somatic healing, you learn to respect your body's knowledge. You know that every suffering has a narrative, and every stress has a purpose. These are not only bodily symptoms to be eliminated, but messages to be comprehended. With each mindful moment, you develop a stronger connection with yourself, learning to listen to and react to your body's needs with compassion and care.

The trip is not always easy. You may come across stormy oceans of suppressed emotions or mountains of opposition. Nonetheless, with mindfulness as your guide, you muster the fortitude to confront these problems. You learn to tolerate discomfort, breathe through suffering, and accept vulnerability. This opens the door to metamorphosis, enabling the healing process to progress organically and at its own time.

Mindfulness in somatic healing is a dance of awareness and acceptance. It is the discipline of being completely present with whatever emerges, without judgement or expectation. As you include mindfulness into your somatic practices, you realise that healing is a journey, not a destination—a journey that returns you to yourself, entire and complete.

Mindful meditation and body scanning.

Close your eyes and take a deep breath. Allow the oxygen to fill your lungs, then gently exhale, feeling the tension leave your body. You are about to begin on a journey of mindfulness meditation and body scanning, which will help you get a better awareness of your physical and mental condition.

Start at the crown of your head. Observe any feelings, such as a tiny pressure or the air brushing your skin. There is no need to alter anything; just observe. As you pay attention to each portion of your body, you may notice regions of tension or pain. Acknowledge them without passing judgement, and breathe into these gaps.

Allow your gaze to go down to your forehead, eyes, cheeks, and jaw. If your mind wanders, gently bring it back to the present moment and the experience of being in your body. This is the core of mindfulness: being totally present in the moment.

As you continue your scan, focus on your neck and shoulders, which are common stress points. Inhale deeply, and as you exhale, visualise the stress fading away. Travel down your arms, hands, and fingertips, feeling the vitality inside you throbbing on the surface.

Your quest will lead you to your chest and abdomen. Feel the rise and fall of each breath from the heart of your being. It's a rhythmic dance that keeps you in the present. Descend to your hips, thighs, and feet. With each breath, you grow more anchored and grounded.

This body scan is more than just a relaxation technique; it is a method of self-discovery. Paying attention to your body helps you connect with your inner self. You learn to listen to your body's whispers, treat it with respect, and enjoy the present moment. This is your moment, a haven of peace in the middle of life's turmoil. Embrace, embrace, and take this sensation of serenity with you as you gradually open your eyes and return to the world around you.

How to Practise Body Scanning:

Body scanning is a mindfulness technique in which you pay great attention to various regions of your body to detect any feelings, tension, or pain. Here's a step-by-step instruction to assist you with body scanning:

1. Find a peaceful Space: Select a comfortable and peaceful location where you will not be disturbed. You may choose to lay on your back or sit comfortably on a chair.

2. Begin with Deep Breathing: Close your eyes and take deep breaths. Inhale gently through your nose, letting your belly rise, then exhale through your mouth. Continue breathing until it feels natural and calm.

3. Concentrate on Your Feet: Start the body scan by paying attention to your feet. Feel any feelings, such as warmth, coldness, pressure, or tingling. Do not criticise or attempt to modify these experiences; just watch them.

4. Scan Upwards: Move your concentration gradually up your body, including your ankles, calves, knees, thighs, and hips. Spend a time focusing on each location, noting any feelings or emotions that emerge.

5. Acknowledge Tension: If you notice any regions of tension or discomfort, acknowledge them. Breathe into these locations, and as you exhale, visualise the tension dissipating from your body.

6. Scanning Each Body Part: Continue until you reach the top of your head. Focus on your stomach, chest, back, arms, neck, and face. Take your time and breathe steadily.

7. Finish with Full Awareness: Once you've reached the top of your head, take a couple more deep breaths. Then, focus your awareness on your whole body at once. Feel the weight of your body and the sense of being completely present.

8. Gently Conclude: When you're ready, carefully open your eyes and observe how your whole body feels. Consider any changes in your physical or mental condition.

Remember that the purpose of body scanning is not to relax or alleviate discomfort, but rather to become more aware of your physical feelings and connect with your body in the present moment. With experience, you'll probably discover that body scanning may help you manage stress and improve your overall feeling of wellbeing.

Developing present moment awareness

You find yourself in a universe that is always moving ahead, a river of time that rushes without halt. But inside you, there is a calm, a tranquil spot where each instant is its own cosmos. This is where you will study the practice of building present-moment awareness.

Imagine you're wandering through a garden. With each stride, you're not just moving; you're also feeling the soil under your feet, hearing the rustling of leaves, and watching the dance of light and shadow. You are completely present at this moment.

Now, apply this awareness to your everyday life. Allow your morning coffee to warm you, taste its richness, and smell its welcoming scent. Be there with your coffee, as if nothing else existed. This is the essence of present-moment awareness: immersing oneself in the now.

It's easy to become lost in thoughts of the past or plans for the future, but cultivating present-moment mindfulness helps you anchor yourself in the experience of life. You sense the air in your lungs, the beat of your heart, and the feelings that move over your skin.

This activity is about acknowledgment as well as pleasure. You begin to recognize the beautiful in the everyday and the remarkable in the ordinary. The sound of rain becomes a symphony, the feel of cloth tells a narrative.

However, it is not always about being nice. Being present might include confronting discomfort, admitting suffering, and sitting with grief. Even here, however, appearance carries power. By not turning away, you will learn, develop, and gain strength.

Developing present-moment awareness is similar to growing a muscle. It requires practice, patience, and perseverance. Begin small, with a single breath, stride, or instant. And when you do, you'll notice that life, in all of its tumult and tranquillity, becomes richer, deeper, and much more valuable.

You are not just moving through time; you are experiencing it, one conscious moment at a time. And it is a lovely thing.

Emotional Regulation Techniques

You are in control of your emotions while you navigate the traffic of everyday life. Sometimes it's a nice trip, and sometimes it's bumper-to-bumper tension. Emotional regulation strategies work like a GPS, helping you to successfully regulate your emotions regardless of the road conditions.

First, consider your feelings as passengers. They're along for the journey, but you have control of the steering wheel. Recognizing the voices of wrath and worry in the backseat. said, "I see you, I hear you, but we're not taking that detour." This is self-talk, which allows you to take a step back and view the broader picture.

Next, consider the power of the pause. Feeling frustrated at a red light? Rather than blowing your horn, take a big breath. Count to 10. This is organised breathing, and it's like putting your emotional foot on the brake to slow things down and allow you to think properly.

Then there's the picturesque way to distraction. When emotions are high, switch gears. Concentrate on something else—a podcast, a puzzle, a stroll. It's not running away; it's taking a mental vacation so you can return to your emotions with a new perspective.

Also, consider the reassessment approach. It's similar to wiping your windshield for a clearer perspective. Maybe the car didn't cut you off on purpose; maybe they were hurrying to an emergency. Changing your interpretation of a circumstance might affect how you feel about it.

Finally, remember to check your mirrors with awareness. Stay present. Take in the environment around you, the feel of the steering wheel, and the sound of the engine. It keeps you grounded and stops emotions from taking over your path.

Remember that you are in charge. With these strategies, you'll be able to achieve serenity and balance even in the midst of intense emotional turmoil. Travel safely on your emotional trip.

Identifying and communicating emotions

You are on a journey to better understand and express your emotions, which will lead to a healthier, more balanced you. It all begins with recognizing how you're feeling. Is enjoyment bubbling up within you like a spring, or is worry looming over your thoughts? Naming your feelings is the first stage, similar to placing a label on a map.

Now that you've discovered your feelings, it's time to express them. Imagine your emotions are colours, and you're painting a picture of your inner world. Use words to explain your feelings, as if you were telling someone about a masterpiece you had produced. It's alright if the colours blur and the distinctions aren't always evident; emotions may be complicated.

Remember that expressing your feelings is like opening a window in a stuffy room; it brings in new air and expels the old. If you're feeling happy, spread it like sunlight. If it's sorrowful, let it fall like soft rain. If you're angry, let it out like a gust of wind, but don't let it become a storm.

Sometimes you may have difficulty finding the appropriate words. That's when you may experiment with other means of expression, such as music, painting, or even dancing. When words fail you, use them to express your feelings.

But here's the key: always express your feelings in a manner that respects both yourself and others. Nurture your emotional garden with care, just like a gardener does with plants. Prune the thorns of harmful remarks and nurture the seedlings of constructive conversation.

Identifying and expressing your emotions helps you not only understand yourself better, but also builds bridges with others. It's a talent that requires practice, just like any other. So stick at it, and watch your emotional landscape blossom into something beautiful and understandable.

Managing overpowering sensations.

You're standing in the midst of a storm, with emotions whirling around you like furious winds. It's easy to feel lost, but remember that you have the ability to find peace among the turmoil. Here's how to deal with such overpowering feelings:

First, take a big breath. Feel the air fill your lungs and gently exhale. This simple gesture may serve as a lifeline, anchoring you in the present moment and stopping the tornado of thoughts.

Second, determine what is causing the storm. Is it job, relationships, or just too much on your plate? Pinpointing the source provides a starting point for addressing the issue.

Third, allow yourself to feel. It's alright to feel overwhelmed. Accepting your feelings does not imply weakness; rather, it demonstrates your humanity. Treat yourself with the same compassion that you would show a friend in trouble.

Fourth, separate the hurricane into breezes. Take one thing at a time. When everything seems urgent, prioritise. ask yourself, "What needs my full attention right now?" and concentrate on it.

Fifth, take safety in routines. When emotions are running wild, structure may provide a safe refuge. Set aside time for meals, sleep, and some leisure. It won't stop the storm, but it will help you get through it.

Sixth, interact with others. Share your emotions with someone you trust. Sometimes simply talking about what you're going through will help to lighten the weight and bring in some brightness.

Seventh, remember that storms do not persist forever. The sense of being overwhelmed is just fleeting. With each stride, you get closer to a brighter sky.

Finally, if the storm seems overwhelming, seek expert assistance. There is strength in seeking help, much like locating a beacon that directs ships to safety.

You've got it. One breath, one step, one day at a time. The storm will pass, and you will be stronger for having endured it.

Integrating Mindfulness with Somatic Practices

You're on a journey to find inner peace and balance, and combining mindfulness with somatic practices is like using a map and a compass. Mindfulness is your map, revealing the terrain of your inner experiences. Somatic practices serve as a guide for you while you navigate your body's experiences.

Begin by locating a peaceful area. Sit or lay down comfortably, then shut your eyes. Take a deep breath in, hold it for a time, then exhale gently. Feel the air go through your nose, into your lungs, and out of your body. This is mindfulness: being completely present with your breath.

Now, concentrate on your body. Take note of any regions of tension or ease. Perhaps your shoulders are tense, or your hands are relaxed. This is the somatic part—listening to your body's signals. Do not pass judgement or attempt to alter anything; instead, observe.

As you continue to breathe deeply, see each breath reaching the tight areas of your body. With each breath, imagine the tension melting away like ice in the light. This is how you combine mindfulness with somatic practices—connecting with and soothing your body via mental awareness.

You may practise this integration anywhere, at any time. You may be attentive of your breath and body whether waiting in line, sitting at your computer, or strolling. It is about returning your focus to the present moment and the bodily feelings you are feeling.

This technique enables you to feel more grounded and focused. It's a technique for calming the whirlwind of thoughts and emotions that might occasionally overwhelm you. Integrating mindfulness with somatic activities allows you to live completely in your body as well as your mind.

Remember that this is a practice. The more you practise, the more natural it will become. And as you incorporate these techniques into your everyday life, you'll notice a feeling of serenity and clarity that will help you deal with whatever comes your way.

Daily activities for mindfulness and somatic exercises.

Developing a daily regimen that includes mindfulness and somatic activities may greatly improve your mind-body connection. Here's a simple and efficient program to get you started:

1. To start your day, take a minute to observe your breath and make an aim.

2. Gentle Stretching: Use gentle stretches to wake up your body and relieve any stiffness from sleep.

3. Mindful Breathing: Spend 5-10 minutes concentrating on deep, diaphragmatic breathing to ground yourself for the day ahead.

Midday:

1. Mindful Walking: Take a brief stroll and focus on the feeling of your feet contacting the earth.

2. Body Scan: During your lunch break, do a fast 5-minute body scan, detecting any points of tension and intentionally relaxing them.

Afternoon:

1. Somatic Movements: Use pelvic tilts and shoulder rolls to relieve tension and increase body awareness.

2. Mindful Snack: Eat a small snack consciously, appreciating the tastes and textures while paying attention to your body's hunger signs.

Evening:

1. Reflective Journaling: Reflect on your day, noting any moments of awareness and areas for improvement.

2. Yoga or Tai Chi: Practise yoga or tai chi to harmonise your body and mind while concentrating on the flow of movements.

Before bed:

1. Gratitude Practice: List three things you're thankful for to help change your emphasis to good events.

2. Relaxation Exercise: Finish your day with a relaxation exercise, such as progressive muscle relaxation or guided imagery, to prepare for a good night's sleep.

Remember that consistency and adaptation are essential components of this routine's effectiveness. Feel free to tailor the activities to your schedule and tastes. The objective is to develop a practice of mindfulness and somatic awareness that will benefit your general well-being.

Long-term approaches to emotional wellness.

Long-term methods for emotional health include routines and habits that help you cope with life's pressures and retain a good attitude. Here are a few major strategies:

1. Increase Emotional Intelligence: Learn to understand and regulate your own emotions, as well as perceive and impact the emotions of others.

2. Increase Resilience: Develop the capacity to recover from setbacks. This might include adopting good physical habits, expressing appreciation, and seeking meaning and purpose in life.

3. Create a Support Network: Surround yourself with good, supporting individuals. Strong social relationships may provide comfort and support during difficult times.

4. Practice Mindfulness: Meditation or yoga may help you remain grounded in the present moment and minimise stress.

5. Maintain Physical Health: Regular exercise, a healthy diet, and enough sleep are all necessary for emotional well-being.

6. Seek Professional Help When Necessary: Consult a therapist or counsellor for advice and support.

7. Establish Boundaries: Learn to say no and restrict your time and emotional energy.

8. Pursue Hobbies and Interests: Participate in activities that make you happy and fulfilled.

9. Develop a good Mindset: Focus on good ideas and attitudes while challenging negative thinking habits.

10. Learn Stress Management Techniques: Create skills for dealing with stress, such as deep breathing, progressive muscle relaxation, or visualisation.

By incorporating these tactics into your daily routine, you may improve your mental health and general quality of life. Remember that emotional wellness is a process, not a destination, and it demands constant attention and care.

Part IV: Advance Topics in Somatic Trauma Healing

Neuroplasticity and Healing

Imagine you are holding a lump of clay in your hands. This clay symbolises the brain. Your brain, like clay, can morph and adapt to new shapes. Neuroplasticity refers to your brain's capacity to rearrange itself and generate new connections.

Now consider a period when you learnt a new skill, such as riding a bike or playing an instrument. It was difficult at first, but with time and practice, it grew easier. That is an example of neuroplasticity in action. Each time you trained, your brain formed new pathways and strengthened the connections required to perfect the skill.

Neuroplasticity, however, is more than simply learning new things; it also involves mending. If you've ever been injured or traumatised, your brain may employ neuroplasticity to recover and compensate for lost abilities. For example, if one region of the brain is destroyed, another area may take up the missing function, similar to rerouting traffic when a road is blocked.

You may boost neuroplasticity by doing brain-challenging tasks. This might be everything from learning a new language to completing riddles. Physical activity, proper diet, and appropriate sleep all contribute to a healthy brain that is ready to adapt and recover.

Remember that your brain is not permanent; it is malleable, like the clay in your hands. With time, effort, and the correct activities, you can mould your brain to improve learning and healing. So keep pushing yourself, being interested, and giving your brain the attention it needs to grow. Neuroplasticity is your brain's intrinsic ability to strengthen itself in the face of adversity.

How the brain reacts to somatic treatment.

Imagine your brain as a garden. A garden can transform with the correct care and circumstances, and so can your brain with somatic therapy. This treatment, like the gardener's tools, may help modify the way your brain operates.

When you go through somatic therapy, you concentrate on your body's feelings and motions. This attentiveness assists your brain in making new connections. It is similar to sowing fresh seeds in your garden. With time and effort, these seeds sprout, and your brain learns new ways to react to emotions and stress.

Somatic therapy may have an influence on brain regions involved for emotional control, such as the prefrontal cortex. This area of the brain functions as a command centre for emotion regulation. When it is reinforced via treatment, you may find it easier to remain cool and collected in previously upsetting circumstances.

Another region of your brain, the amygdala, functions similarly to an alert system. It responds to both fear and stress. Somatic treatment may help decrease the sensitivity of this alert. It's like setting a sprinkler system to water the plants just so, neither too little nor too much.

Somatic therapy may also help to regulate your autonomic nervous system, which governs things like your heartbeat and breathing without your conscious thought. It's like the garden's ecology establishing balance, ensuring that everything runs properly.

By participating in somatic activities, you may help your brain remodel itself. This process, known as neuroplasticity, indicates that your brain is constantly capable of changing. With each somatic exercise, you nourish your brain's garden, promoting development and healing.

In a nutshell, somatic therapy helps your brain evolve by forming new connections and strengthening old ones. It's an effective technique to boost your emotional health and well-being by training your brain new patterns of reaction and resilience.

Real-world examples of neuroplasticity

Neuroplasticity is the brain's extraordinary capacity to rearrange itself by generating new neural connections over time. This flexibility enables the brain to compensate for damage and sickness, as well as react to new learning opportunities. Here are some case studies that demonstrate neuroplasticity in action.

1. Neuroplasticity and Workplace Performance: Maurice Forget and Noémie Le Pertel studied how neuroplasticity affects learning and memory in the workplace. They discovered that cognitive training, brain stimulation, and mindfulness may boost neuroplasticity, which leads to better work performance.

2. London Taxi Drivers: Eleanor Maguire's research found that rigorous training in spatial navigation led to increased hippocampus size. The hippocampus is crucial in memory and spatial cognition, and the research found that severe learning events caused the brain to structurally alter.

3. Neurogenesis: Neuroplasticity includes the generation of new neurons, in addition to creating new connections. This process has been seen across all mammalian species, demonstrating the brain's adaptability and evolution.

4. Sensory Map Enlargement: Enlarging cortical sensory maps, which process sensory information, has been linked to perceptual benefits. This implies that when we acquire and practise new abilities, the brain regions associated with those talents might physically develop.

These case studies show that neuroplasticity is a continuous process that may cause considerable changes in the brain's structure and functionality. The capacity of the brain to rewire itself is a tremendous tool for development and adaptability, whether it is used to acquire new abilities, adjust to new circumstances, or heal from damage. Neuroplasticity guarantees that our brains are dynamic, developing in response to our experiences and activities. It is crucial to how we learn, remember, and interact with our surroundings.

Somatic Therapy and Other Approaches

Somatic therapy is a comprehensive therapeutic method that stresses the relationship between mind and body. It is founded on the belief that emotional and psychological stress may appear physically in the body. This style of treatment tries to help people release tension, stress, and trauma by concentrating on body sensations and integrating physical movements into their recovery.

What Does Somatic Therapy Involve?

Somatic therapy combines conversation therapy and physical approaches. During sessions, therapists help clients investigate their bodily feelings and relate them to emotional experiences. Deep breathing, relaxation exercises, meditation, dancing, and even soft touch or massage are all possible techniques. The objective is to assist the client become more aware of their body and learn how to release any tension that may be contributing to their mental health problems.

Somatic Therapy Treats These Conditions

Somatic therapy is very useful for treating illnesses such as post-traumatic stress disorder (PTSD), anxiety, sadness, grieving, and stress-related difficulties. It is also used to boost self-esteem and solve difficulties of trust and intimacy.

How does somatic therapy work?

The treatment works by using the body's inherent healing capabilities. For example, while discussing a traumatic situation, a therapist may observe a client's clenched fists and investigate the bodily sensations. By concentrating on releasing the tightness in the fists, the client may begin to loosen the emotional grasp of the memories.

Other Modalities in Somatic Therapy

Somatic therapy is divided into many kinds, each with their unique emphasis and procedures. This includes:

Sensorimotor Psychotherapy combines bodily awareness with psychotherapy to treat trauma and attachment disorders.

- **The Hakomi Method** combines Western psychology and Eastern philosophy, with an emphasis on mindfulness and the body's knowledge.
- **Bioenergetic Analysis**: This technique uses bodily movement, analysis, and relationship dynamics to comprehend and release energy that has been imprisoned in the body.
- **Biodynamic Psychotherapy:** Uses physical massage to interact with the body's energy processes.
- **Brainspotting:** Uses eye position to process and release unresolved trauma.

Effectiveness of Somatic Therapy.

While somatic therapy is still gaining popularity, many people believe it is an effective technique to treat difficulties that standard talk therapy may not entirely resolve. It provides a holistic approach that recognizes the intricate relationship between the physical body and mental well-being.

Integrating somatic therapy with psychotherapy, EMDR, and other techniques.

Integrating somatic therapy with psychotherapy and Eye Movement Desensitization and Reprocessing (EMDR) entails integrating these treatments to speed up the healing process for those struggling with trauma and other psychological difficulties. This integration is founded on the notion that the mind and body are inextricably linked, and that treating both may result in deeper and more permanent healing.

1. Somatic Therapy and Psychotherapy.

Somatic therapy employs the body's feelings and motions to relieve accumulated tension and trauma. Psychotherapy often entails discussing feelings and experiences. Therapists may combine somatic treatments such as mindful movement or breathwork with cognitive conversations to assist clients in processing and releasing emotional suffering.

2. EMDR and Somatic Awareness

EMDR is a systematic treatment for processing and integrating traumatic experiences. It entails reliving traumatic experiences while concentrating on a kind of bilateral sensory input, such as side-to-side eye movements. Integrating somatic therapy with EMDR requires therapists to pay attention to the client's body reactions throughout sessions, employing somatic signals to guide the process and improve the therapeutic impact.

Benefits of Integration:

The combination of these medicines may provide various advantages:

- **Comprehensive Treatment:** It takes into account both the psychological and physiological components of trauma.

- **Improved Processing:** Somatic awareness may aid in the processing of traumatic memories during EMDR.

- **Increased Self-Regulation:** Clients learn to recognize and control their bodily reactions to stress and trauma.

How It is Done

In practice, a therapist may start with typical EMDR procedures and subsequently add somatic therapies. For example, if a client feels physically tight when remembering a memory, the therapist may employ somatic methods to assist the client remain present and grounded, allowing for more effective memory processing.

Training for Therapists

Therapists who are interested in this integrated approach often get further training in both somatic therapy and EMDR to guarantee that both modalities may be used safely and successfully.

- Combining somatic therapy, psychotherapy, and Eye Movement Desensitization and Reprocessing (EMDR) improves the healing process for those struggling with trauma and other psychological disorders. This integration is founded on the notion that the mind and body are inextricably linked, and that treating both may result in deeper and more permanent healing.

Somatic Therapy and Psychotherapy.

Somatic therapy employs the body's feelings and motions to relieve accumulated tension and trauma. Psychotherapy often entails discussing feelings and experiences. Therapists may combine somatic treatments such as mindful movement or breathwork with cognitive conversations to assist clients in processing and releasing emotional suffering.

EMDR and Somatic Awareness

EMDR is a systematic treatment for processing and integrating traumatic experiences. It entails reliving traumatic experiences while concentrating on a kind of bilateral sensory input, such as side-to-side eye movements. Integrating somatic therapy with EMDR requires therapists to pay attention to the client's body reactions throughout sessions, employing somatic signals to guide the process and improve the therapeutic impact.

Benefits of Integration:

The combination of these medicines may provide various advantages:

- **Comprehensive Treatment**: It takes into account both the psychological and physiological components of trauma.

- **Improved Processing**: Somatic awareness may aid in the processing of traumatic memories during EMDR.

- **Increased Self-Regulation:** Clients learn to recognize and control their bodily reactions to stress and trauma.

How It is Done

In practice, a therapist may start with typical EMDR procedures and subsequently add somatic therapies. For example, if a client feels physically tight when remembering a memory, the therapist may employ somatic methods to assist the client remain present and grounded, allowing for more effective memory processing.

Training for Therapists

Therapists who are interested in this integrated approach often get further training in both somatic therapy and EMDR to guarantee that both modalities may be used safely and successfully.

When to employ mixed approaches?

Combined therapeutic techniques, which combine somatic therapy with psychotherapy, EMDR, and other modalities, are especially useful for addressing complicated mental health disorders that do not respond to a single type of treatment. This integrative technique is most successful when dealing with complicated situations that include both psychological and physiological components.

When to Consider Combined Approaches:

- **Complex Trauma:** When a person has undergone several traumatic incidents, particularly throughout childhood, it may lead to illnesses such as PTSD.

- **persistent Conditions**: For long-term mental health problems such persistent depression, anxiety disorders, or personality disorders that persist after regular therapy.

- **Multifactorial Etiology**: When a condition's underlying causes are multifaceted, encompassing biological, psychological, and social elements.

- **Treatment.-Resistant Cases:** When people do not react to standard therapies such as medicine or psychotherapy.

Advantages of Combined Approaches:

- **Holistic Treatment:** Addresses both mind and body for a more thorough approach.

- **Personalized Care:** Therapists may customise the mix of therapy to meet the specific requirements of each patient.

- **Increased Efficacy:** Research suggests that combination therapies are more successful than single modalities, especially for specific diseases such as significant depression and anxiety.

Combining Somatic Therapy with Psychotherapy may improve self-awareness and emotional processing for clients.

- **Psychotherapy and EMDR**: Integrating EMDR may help clients process painful memories more profoundly, whilst psychotherapy allows them to explore and comprehend their experiences.

- **Pharmacotherapy with Psychotherapy**: Medication may help stabilise mood or anxiety symptoms, enabling clients to participate more completely in psychotherapy.

Practitioners should have enough training in each modality to guarantee safe and successful integration.

- **Client Preferences:** Some clients may prefer one therapy over another, and their preferences should be addressed.

- **Cultural Sensitivity:** Therapists should be mindful of the cultural impacts on their clients' sickness experiences and treatment choices.

Cultural Considerations for Somatic Healing

Cultural factors in somatic therapy are important because they acknowledge that people's experiences with their bodies and emotions are heavily impacted by their cultural origins. Somatic healing, which focuses on the link between the body and mind, must be tailored to respect and embrace other cultures' beliefs, traditions, and values.

Understanding Cultural Context

Every culture has its own concept of health, disease, and healing. What is considered a symptom of disease in one culture may be seen as a sign of spiritual enlightenment in another. Somatic therapists must be aware of these distinctions in order to deliver successful and courteous therapy.

Cultural Sensitivity in Therapy.

Therapists should provide a secure environment in which clients feel understood and appreciated, regardless of ethnic origin. This includes being willing to learn about the client's cultural identity and how it affects their perception of recovery.

Integrating Cultural Practices

Many cultures have ancient body-based healing traditions, such as dancing, ceremonial motions, and specialised types of touch. Integrating these techniques into somatic therapy may improve the healing process and make it more relevant to the client.

Addressing Cultural Trauma.

Cultural trauma, such as that caused by colonialism, racism, or forced migration, may have physiological consequences. Therapists must be prepared to handle these difficulties in a sympathetic and helpful manner.

Language & Communication

Language difficulties may impede somatic healing. Therapists should ensure that they can successfully interact with clients and offer interpreters to fill any gaps.

Training & Education

Therapists should seek continual education to better grasp the cultural aspects of somatic healing. This involves instruction on cultural competence and humility.

Collaboration among Cultural Experts

Working with cultural experts or healers may provide therapists significant insights and help them approach somatic therapy in a culturally acceptable manner.

Understanding trauma in different groups.

Understanding trauma in varied groups necessitates acknowledging that trauma may present differently across cultures, ethnicities, genders, and socioeconomic origins. Trauma is not a one-size-fits-all experience; it is influenced by a wide range of elements, including cultural history, personal identity, and the socioeconomic environment in which an individual lives.

1. Cultural History and Trauma

Cultural history has a tremendous impact on how trauma is perceived and articulated. Communities with a history of oppression or colonialism, for example, may be subjected to collective trauma that lasts generations. This form of trauma may shape how people in these societies perceive and deal with stress and hardship.

2. Race and Trauma

Racial trauma is a kind of stress caused by racial prejudice and violence that one has experienced or seen. It may cause psychiatric symptoms akin to PTSD and have an impact on both people and communities' well-being. Understanding racial trauma is critical to delivering culturally appropriate treatment and support.

3. Gender & Trauma

Gender may also have an impact on how trauma is experienced. Women and gender minorities may experience unique sorts of trauma, such as sexual abuse or gender-based discrimination, necessitating particular knowledge and therapeutic techniques.

4. Socioeconomic Status and Trauma

Access to trauma-coping services may be influenced by socioeconomic position. Those from poorer socioeconomic backgrounds may have less options for help and healing, rendering them more exposed to the long-term consequences of traumatic occurrences.

5. Language & Trauma

Language limitations may have an influence on how people express and address trauma. Non-native speakers may struggle to describe their experiences, and therapists must be proficient at communicating across language barriers in order to give effective help.

Trauma-informed care

Trauma-informed care is a strategy that recognizes the many forms of trauma. It entails comprehending the presence of trauma and its varied cultural forms, identifying the signs and symptoms of trauma in clients, and reacting by incorporating trauma knowledge into policies, procedures, and practices.

Making somatic techniques more culturally relevant.

Adapting somatic practices for cultural relevance entails modifying body-centred treatment procedures to meet the varying beliefs, values, and traditions of other cultures. Somatic practices, which encompass treatments such as dance, movement, and mindfulness, emphasise the body's involvement in psychological health. When these procedures are culturally adapted, they become more successful while also respecting the individual's heritage.

Cultural Relevance in Somatic Practices.

Cultural relevance refers to making treatment relevant and accessible to persons from diverse cultural backgrounds. It is necessary to comprehend and integrate the client's cultural norms, language, and worldview into the therapy process.

Steps for cultural adaptation:

1. Research and Understanding: Therapists must learn about their clients' cultures, including traditional healing traditions, communication patterns, and attitudes regarding mental health.

2. Client Collaboration: Engaging clients in a discourse about their cultural preferences and experiences ensures that treatment is tailored to their needs.

3. Integrating Traditional Practices: Many cultures have developed practices that incorporate bodily awareness, such as yoga or tai chi. Integrating them into somatic therapy may improve the healing process.

4. Language Considerations: Using the client's chosen language or offering translation services may aid in efficient communication.

5. resolving Cultural Trauma: Recognizing and compassionately resolving trauma caused by cultural events such as racism or colonialism is critical.

6. Continuous input: Regularly soliciting input from clients allows therapists to alter their approach to better meet the client's cultural demands.

Cultural Adaptation Benefits:

- **Increased Comfort and Trust**: Respecting clients' cultural identity leads to more engagement in treatment.

- **Improved Outcomes:** Culturally relevant therapy is frequently more successful since it connects with the client's life experience.

- **Increased Accessibility:** Adapting methods makes somatic therapy available to a broader spectrum of individuals, encouraging inclusion.

Cultural adaptation challenges include avoiding oversimplification and stereotyping due to the complexity of cultures.

- **Training**: Therapists may need further training to effectively adapt treatments for cultural relevance.
- **Balancing Universality and Specificity:** Somatic concepts are universal, but their implementation must be culturally appropriate.

Conclusion

The future of somatic trauma healing

The future of somatic trauma healing looks promising as it continues to evolve and integrate with other therapeutic modalities. Here are some key aspects that are shaping its future:

1. Integration with Technology:
Advancements in technology, such as virtual reality and biofeedback, are being explored to enhance somatic practices. These tools can help individuals become more aware of their bodily responses and learn to regulate them in real-time.

2. Research and Evidence-Based Practice:
There is a growing emphasis on research to establish the efficacy of somatic approaches. As

evidence accumulates, somatic therapy may become more widely accepted and utilised within mainstream mental health services.

3. Global and Cultural Expansion:

Somatic therapy is expanding globally, with practitioners adapting techniques to be culturally relevant and sensitive. This expansion is crucial for making somatic healing accessible to diverse populations.

4. Interdisciplinary Collaboration:

Collaboration between somatic practitioners and professionals from other disciplines, such as neuroscience and psychology, is leading to a more comprehensive understanding of trauma and its treatment.

5. Focus on Prevention and Education:

There is an increasing focus on using somatic practices not just for healing but also for prevention. Educational programs are teaching individuals somatic awareness and self-regulation skills from an early age.

6. Community and Collective Healing:

Somatic therapy is being applied to community settings, addressing collective trauma and fostering resilience in groups affected by shared experiences.

7. Personalised and Holistic Approaches:

The future of somatic trauma healing is moving towards more personalised care, considering the individual's unique history, circumstances, and needs for a holistic approach to recovery.

8. Accessibility and Affordability:

Efforts are being made to make somatic therapy more accessible and affordable, including online resources and group therapy options.

Encouragement for continued learning and practice

Continued learning and practice are key to personal growth and mastery in any field. Here's a little encouragement to keep you motivated on your journey:

Keep Exploring:

Every step you take in learning something new opens up a world of possibilities. Remember, the more you learn, the more you realise there's so much more to discover.

Embrace Challenges:

Challenges are not roadblocks; they're stepping stones. Each one is an opportunity to grow stronger and become more skilled.

Celebrate Progress:

No matter how small, every bit of progress is worth celebrating. Acknowledge your achievements along the way.

Stay Curious:

Curiosity is the fuel for learning. Ask questions, seek answers, and never lose the wonder that drives you forward.

Be Patient:

Mastery doesn't happen overnight. Be patient with yourself and trust in the process of gradual improvement.

Connect with Others:

Learning is more enriching when shared. Connect with others who can support you, teach you, and learn from you.

Find Joy in Practice:

Practice doesn't have to be a chore. Find the joy in honing your skills and take pleasure in the practice itself.

Remember Your 'Why':

Whenever you feel discouraged, remind yourself why you started. Your personal 'why' can be a powerful motivator to keep going.

Stay Flexible:

Be open to adapting your methods and trying new approaches. Flexibility can lead to breakthroughs in learning.

Trust Yourself:

Believe in your ability to learn and improve. You have everything it takes to achieve your goals.

Keep pushing forward, stay dedicated, and remember that every expert was once a beginner. Your potential is limitless, and your journey is uniquely yours. Embrace it fully, and enjoy where it takes you. You've got this!